THE PAGAN
HEART
OF TODAY'S CULTURE

CHRISTIAN ANSWERS TO HARD QUESTIONS

Christian Interpretations of Genesis 1

Christianity and the Role of Philosophy

Creation, Evolution, and Intelligent Design

Did Adam Exist?

How Can I Know for Sure?

How Did Evil Come into the World?

The Morality of God in the Old Testament

The Pagan Heart of Today's Culture

Should You Believe in God?

Was Jesus Really Born of a Virgin?

Peter A. Lillback and Steven T. Huff, Series Editors

THE PAGAN
HEART
OF TODAY'S CULTURE

PETER JONES

PHILADELPHIA, PENNSYLVANIA

P&R
PUBLISHING
P.O. BOX 817 • PHILLIPSBURG • NEW JERSEY 08865-0817

Westminster Seminary Press, LLC, a Pennsylvania limited-liability company, is a wholly owned subsidiary of Westminster Theological Seminary.

This work is a co-publication of P&R Publishing and Westminster Seminary Press, LLC.

Only Two Religions, Peter Jones's video series with Ligonier Ministries, complements and expands the content of *The Pagan Heart of Today's Culture*. To order *Only Two Religions*, visit www.Ligonier.org or call (800) 435-4343. UPC Codes: DVD—881658004370, CD—881658004363.

ISBN: 978-1-62995-087-7 (pbk)
ISBN: 978-1-62995-088-4 (ePub)
ISBN: 978-1-62995-089-1 (Mobi)

Printed in the United States of America

Library of Congress Control Number: 2014937005

THIS BOOKLET EXAMINES the spiritual heart of our culture through a prism of *isms*. Though *ism* words can be daunting, they also can be helpful because they are precise. This booklet argues that three seemingly unrelated *isms* (or worldviews)—postmodernism, Gnosticism, and polytheism—form a constructive lens through which we can understand what is sometimes called the New Spirituality. Readers may well ask what meaningful connection could exist between the worldwide ancient religion of polytheism, the first-through-fourth-century Christian heresy of Gnosticism, and the contemporary philosophy of postmodernism. To find out, read on! These three ways of thinking have become strangely connected. Together they help explain the nature of today's pagan worldview and its opposition to the truth of the gospel. To understand the interconnectedness of the three *isms*, we first must look at each one separately.

Before we move on

+ As you begin this booklet, what do you already know about polytheism, Gnosticism, and postmodernism? Are you aware of any ways in which these ideologies influence you or people with whom you have contact?

+ What will the author be arguing about these three *isms*? Why is his argument important to Christians?

POSTMODERNISM

Being a postmodern has very little to do with sporting tattoos, wearing grungy clothes, or adopting an easygoing nature. Literally, the postmodern is someone who has dispensed with the modern. In philosophical terms, *modern* describes a two-hundred-year period of intellectual history, called the Enlightenment, in which human reason was held to be the only arbiter of truth. That period was bookended by two symbolic "falls," one in 1789 and the other in 1989.

On July 14, 1789, the Bastille Prison in Paris fell, representing the demise of the combined despotic authority of the Crown and the church. Though this dreaded place of confinement actually contained only seven prisoners, its fall was mere symbolic "political theater," since the incident served to launch the French Revolution. Talk about "political theater"! On November 10, 1793, revolutionaries placed a bust of the goddess Reason on the high altar in the cathedral of Notre Dame de Paris. Rationalism had triumphed over religious superstition. This rationalist movement was the first great apostasy from Christianity in the modern era. One of the fathers of the French Revolution, Voltaire, gave to the Revolution the famous phrase *Écrasez l'infâme*: "Crush the horrid thing." The "horrid thing" was the superstition of Christianity. From then on, skepticism of all things spiritual was considered a sign of true intelligence, reason the sole measure of reality and the basis for human progress. Modernism even entered the church, denying the supernatural, the miracles, and the divinity of Christ. The success of modernism led many Western thinkers in the nineteenth and twentieth centuries to expect that the twenty-first century would see the full flowering of secularism and the disappearance of irrational religion. They were wrong. Believe it or not, scholars now speak of the *postsecular age*.[1] Postsecularism "does not accept that reason must rule out religion."[2]

The "fall" that brought a close to the modern period was the fall of the Berlin Wall in 1989, symbolizing the collapse of materialism and of atheistic, secular Marxism. What brought down the great edifice of rational Enlightenment and modernist culture? It was postmodernism, which, though it rejects the truth claims of Christianity, also undermines "[all] absolutist explanations of reality, [including atheistic] Marxism."[3] The postmodern laser gun was aimed not only at Christianity but also at the *ideology* of secularism, in "a rage against humanism and the Enlightenment legacy."[4]

BEFORE WE MOVE ON

+ What beliefs characterize modernism? How can these beliefs be seen in the unfolding of the French Revolution, starting with the fall of the Bastille?

+ How did modernism affect the church? Why is this abandonment of Christian orthodoxy a natural consequence of embracing modernism?

+ What beliefs characterize postmodernism? What ideologies does it oppose?

+ How was the fall of the Berlin Wall a symbolic deathblow to modernism?

"Postmodern deconstruction" deconstructs *any* confidence in absolute truth.[5] "There is no empirical 'fact' that is not already theory-laden, and there is no logical argument or formal principle that is *a priori* certain."[6] Interestingly, the Christian apologist Cornelius Van Til of Westminster Theological Seminary also said that facts were never neutral. If postmoderns and Reformed apologists say the same thing, it is doubtless true![7] Unlike the modern mind, which merely assumed that reality is objectively ordered via human reason, and the Christian mind, which assumed it to be regulated by God's will, the postmodern mind rejects all objective truths and true personhood. All that it can propose are blurred and amorphous partial truths—except in one instance. The postmodern critique of human rationalism is reasonable only if it presupposes the rationality of postmodern reasoning.

But this is also circular, since, while denying the possibility of objective truth to modernity, it claims to make an objectively true statement that rational humanism lacks objectivity.[8] Postmodernism is thus guilty of the same circular reasoning of which it accuses Enlightenment rationalism.

The postmodern critique has stuck partly because secularism has earned a dark reputation, in spite of its optimism for humanity's future. After all, instead of utopia, it produced two devastating world wars, the threat of nuclear annihilation, dehumanizing industrialization, and material consumerism, not to mention looming ecological disasters. The West has begun to lose faith not in religion but rather in autonomous human reason. Postmodern intellectuals now recoil from "the embarrassing intolerance of atheism."[9] Tolerance has become one of the great values to be respected, even the tolerance of religion and spirituality.

BEFORE WE MOVE ON

+ In what way do postmodernists agree with the Christian apologist Cornelius Van Til? How are they both responding to modernism's mistaken belief about human rationalism?

+ In what way do Christians and postmodernists fundamentally *disagree*?

+ How is postmodernism circular in its critique of human rationalism? Even so, why has its critique resonated with many people? What makes postmodernism seem likely to avoid modernism's failures?

But can we live in a world lying in ruins, deconstructed by postmodernism? A contemporary philosopher, David Harvey, ends his magisterial study on postmodernism with the following observation: "Postmodernity is undergoing a subtle evolution, perhaps reaching a point of self-dissolution into something different. But what?"[10]

To this question—and to theologian Alister McGrath's similar question: "What will replace atheism?"[11]—my answer would be: Atheism (no God) will be replaced by *pan*theism (everything is god). *Logos* ("word") will be replaced by *mythos* ("myth"). This spiritual, nonrational answer arises from the heart of postmodernism. Jacques Derrida, hailed as the creator of postmodern deconstructionism, argued that the purpose of that deconstruction was to "deconstruct the dualisms and hierarchies embedded in Western thinking"—such as good-evil, mind-body, male-female, truth-fiction. These "false polarities," he claimed, "must be deconstructed."[12] Such a rejection of the opposites is in fact, as we will see, a fundamental aspect of religious paganism, so that postmodern philosophy fits surprisingly well with the religious yearnings for the morality and spirituality of inclusion—pantheistic "all is one" wholeness. Theologian Kevin Vanhoozer agrees. Arguing in terms of literary theory, the point at which postmodernism began its critique of philosophy, Vanhoozer notes that the postmodern philosophers Roland Barthes and Jacques Derrida are

> counter-theologians: there is nothing outside the play of writing, nothing that guarantees that our words refer to the world. The loss of a transcendent signifier—Logos—[along with the death of God] thus follows hard upon the death of the author. . . . With the death of the author and the rejection of the autonomous text, the reader is born. . . . With the birth of the reader, the divine has been relocated: the postmodern era is more comfortable thinking of God not as the transcendent Author but as the immanent Spirit.[13]

Simply put, God, the omniscient author, had died, so no one now knows the plot. If there is no ultimate meaning to the world (since

God, the ultimate author of meaning, is dead), then the author of any text has no access to its meaning. Meaning can be created only subjectively by the reader. But note the spiritual implications. Any individual reader has direct, mysterious-mystical access to "the Spirit." This, as we will see, is paganism in a nutshell. The deconstructed world will be put back together again not by reason but by "myth" or "unreason," as *The Seduction of Unreason*, the title of a recent book on modern philosophy, indicates.[14]

BEFORE WE MOVE ON

✦ What is paganism?

✦ What purpose is foundational to deconstructionism? How might this fit into the pantheistic view that "all is one"?

✦ Deconstructionism first arose in the field of literary theory, and postmodernism holds that the reader personally and subjectively creates a text's meaning. According to Kevin Vanhoozer, how does this prioritize the reader over the author? In a theological sense, how does this "relocate" the divine?

✦ How is the reader's access to the "immanent Spirit" a reflection of pagan beliefs?

Contemporary sociologist Christopher Partridge observes:[15] "The whole thrust of Enlightenment secularism ... has prepare[d] the ground for spiritual and mystical religion."[16] He sees secularism and pagan spirituality as kissing cousins—or, as progressive spiritualists would say, "Enlightenment ... is a necessary stage in the evolution of the human mind."[17] Partridge notes that "we are witnessing a return to a form of magical culture, ... a significant religio-cultural shift happening in the 'real world.'"[18]

The great expert and proponent of interfaith, earth-worshiping religion, Huston Smith, says this as clearly as anyone else.[19] Believ-

THE PAGAN HEART OF TODAY'S CULTURE

ing postmodernism to be provisional, only a stage in human development, he predicts that it is causing humanity to return to the *Perennial Philosophy* (see below): a coded term, used by a certain number of elite thinkers, for the age-old pagan belief in the divinity of the human-natural world. It is the underground well that feeds each religious stream.[20] Perennialism is now emerging aboveground. Prince Charles, Patron of the Temenos Academy, dedicated to the central ideas of the Perennial Philosophy, declares: "Only this great Tradition, in its sacralization of Nature, will solve the environmental crisis of the twenty-first century."[21] Only the pantheistic worship of Nature will save us.

A generation ago, the Christian theologian Francis Schaeffer predicted the massive invasion of Eastern spirituality into the West. "Pantheism will be pressed as the only answer to ecological problems and will be one more influence in the West's becoming increasingly Eastern in its thinking; . . . the Eastern religions will be to Christianity a new, dangerous, Gnosticism."[22] Which leads us to the next *ism*.

In spite of the political slogans of forward-looking hope and change, of beating back the forces of old-fashioned prejudice and tradition, many of the leading "progressive" forces actually believe that the pagan past will save us. This postsecular mystical search for meaning in the nonrational is to be observed in the return to the modern world of the ancient religious system known as Gnosticism.

BEFORE WE MOVE ON

+ What is the Perennial Philosophy? How is it a form of pantheism? How might postmodernism be preparing the way for this philosophy?

+ In what ways is paganism seen as being a possible source of salvation?

GNOSTICISM

Gnosticism proposes a search for the self, not in scriptural revelation or in reason, but within one's own self via mystical trance. *Gnosis* in Greek means "knowledge," but not just any kind of knowledge. It is knowledge in the sense of direct "experience," that is, experience of the self as "divine." Gnosticism thus has deep connections with various aspects of mystical Judaism, Persian (Iranian) and Zoroastrian traditions, Greek Hellenistic traditions, and the imperial mystery religions.

A perfect example comes from one of the forty-seven recently discovered (in 1945) ancient Gnostic texts in Egypt, namely, the Gospel of Thomas. Though some liberal scholars try to claim that Thomas is the first expression of the faith of Jesus and belongs in the Christian canon, as we will see below, it becomes manifestly clear that Thomas is in direct opposition to the books of the New Testament canon. I have pointed this out in a book-length study.[23]

In the Gospels of the New Testament, which were written by the earliest followers of Jesus in the middle or toward the later part of the first century A.D., Jesus asks his disciples to tell him what people say about him. The popular answers miss the mark, but the correct answer is given by Peter through divine revelation from the Father: "You are the Christ, the Son of the living God" (Matt. 16:16).

In the Gnostic Gospel of Thomas, probably put together toward the end of the second century A.D. as a "pious Gnostic fiction,"[24] the very opposite is said.[25] In a polemic against the early church, Peter is incorrectly made to say that Jesus is merely "a righteous angel." Only Thomas understands who Jesus truly is, but in a strange and unexpected way. The Thomas of history says to Jesus in John's Gospel, "My Lord and my God!" (John 20:28). This false Gnostic Thomas says:

"Master, I am incapable of saying what you are like." The Jesus of John's Gospel promises blessing to all who believe what Thomas has just confessed (John 20:29). The reply of Jesus in the Gospel of Thomas is quite different. Jesus says: "I am not your master." We are clearly dealing here with two quite contradictory descriptions of Jesus.

Then the Gnostic Jesus takes Thomas to one side and tells him three secrets. When Thomas returns, the other disciples ask him what Jesus said. Thomas refuses to tell them because he knows that "they will stone him." This is a clear reference to the Jewish penalty for blasphemy, for making oneself God. What does this mean? Jesus will not allow Thomas to call him "master" because Thomas has "drunk from the bubbling stream." Jesus further declares, "He who drinks from my mouth will become like me. I will become he, and the things that are hidden will be revealed."[26] Thomas, called Didymus, which means "twin," is the true Gnostic who, as the twin of Jesus, knows himself to be divine, like Jesus. Here the Creator-creature distinction of biblical revelation is utterly destroyed.

As an "objective historian," Elaine Pagels, who blends Buddhism with her version of Christianity,[27] attempted to rehabilitate the Gnostic "Christians" by portraying them as forgotten heroes of an old class war between the politically motivated orthodox patriarchal bishops and their hapless spiritual victims. She presents Gnosticism as "a wider valid expression of Christianity,"[28] and Gnostic gospels as complementary to the canonical ones. Thomas seemed to fit that agenda to a T. But Jesus of Thomas, in addition to teaching the Gnostic Thomas that he is divine, makes a clearly pantheistic or polytheistic statement:[29] "It is I who am the All. From me did the All come forth.... Split a piece of wood, and I am there. Lift up a stone and you will find me there."[30] Such a view of God is clearly pantheistic and Oneist (that is, paganly monist) and is typical of the entire Gnostic system of belief. The most-respected experts on ancient Gnosticism are two German scholars—Hans Jonas[31] and Kurt Rudolph.[32] Neither sees Gnosticism as Christian. For Jonas, Gnosticism is an ancient form of modern existentialism. For Rudolph, Gnosticism is an independent world religion, not a narrowly limited Christian heresy. He argues that Gnosticism was "a parasite prosper[ing] on the soil of a host religion."[33]

BEFORE WE MOVE ON

+ What quest lies at the heart of Gnosticism? How does this make Gnosticism similar to postmodernism?

+ How is Thomas in the Gospel of Thomas a Gnostic figure? What does he "know" about Jesus? What does he know about himself?

+ What examples does the author give of differences between the Gospel of Thomas and the four historical Gospels? Why do Christians reject the Gospel of Thomas?

+ Why do two experts on ancient Gnosticism also reject Gnosticism as an expression of Christianity? What other philosophies does Gnosticism resemble?

Though Gnostic thought is radically dualistic in affirming opposition between spirit and matter, regarding the entire material universe as both an illusion and the work of an evil and inferior divine being, yet the individual Gnostic sees no opposition between himself and God, no ontological Creator-creature distinction. The Gnostic is made of the same spiritual stuff as the great "Father of the Totalities" or "the All." This is clearly seen by Rudolph, who describes Gnosticism as "dualism on a monistic background."[34]

Monistic pantheism is not just an interesting theological option among the many religious options out there. It is the *essence* of religious pagan worship of nature, which finally is at the heart of modern interfaith movements. The church father Hippolytus (A.D. 170–236) made that connection long ago. He documented that the Gnostics of his day were interfaith practitioners who sought "the wisdom of the pagans."[35] He noted that "Christian" Gnostics attended the ceremonies of the Isis-worshiping mystery cults in order to understand "the universal mystery."[36] Isis was the Magna Mater, the Great Mother, the spiritual soul of nature.

Here is where you get to full-blown, radical Gnosticism. One of the original, recently found Gnostic texts confirms the testimony of Hippolytus. The Gnostic goddess Sophia declares: "[I] am the one whose image is great in Egypt."[37] Isis, the pagan Egyptian goddess of wisdom and magic, is the one "who is great in Egypt."[38] Who is Isis? She is "the still point of the turning world"[39] who proclaims: "I am Nature, the Universal Mother; . . . single manifestation of all gods and goddesses am I."[40] Even as the postmodern Derrida eliminated the opposites, it is of great interest to note that the supreme goal of paganism through the ages is the joining of the opposites—good-evil, male-female, Creator-creature. This is also true of Gnosticism. The Gnostics called God "the Father of the Totalities," who joins all the opposites. God, often revealed in female form as Sophia, as the Goddess, states: "I am androgynous. [I am both Mother and] Father since [I copulate] with myself."[41]

This juxtaposition of contradictory notions also seeks to express the divine mystery, which is found in pagan texts of all kinds. The reason is that there is a fundamental rejection in all forms of paganism of the Creator-creature distinction, and thus the rejection of all significant distinctions within the creation. The physical creation is an error by a foolish god, Jehovah. Just how radical is ancient Gnosticism?

Consistently, in all the Gnostic texts, the false God who leads believers astray is the Creator God of the Bible.[42] He is called a blind fool and a joke because he thinks that, as Creator, he is the true and living God—"I am the LORD, and there is no other" (Isa. 45:18)—not knowing that the Father of the All is above him. He does not know that Sophia is the "Mother of the Universe."[43] More than that, Jahweh is the devil himself, the great demon who rules over the lowest part of the underworld.[44] Jahweh gets what any other devil deserves—he is cast into hell. Zoe, daughter of Sophia, "shackled [him] and threw him down into Hell, under the abyss."[45]

BEFORE WE MOVE ON

+ The author has introduced the ideas of *pagan monism* and *monistic pantheism*, which eliminate a fundamental distinction between which two things? In what ways is Gnosticism both monistic and dualistic? Why does its dualism matter less than its inherent monism?

+ What examples does the author give of opposites' being joined in Gnosticism and paganism? Do you see any attempts to join opposites in the culture around you?

+ Who is the devil in Gnosticism? What does he not know? What ultimately happens to him? Who are the other key players in this story?

Could this catch on in modern America? It should not surprise us that in 1995 a Roman Catholic theologian, Richard Grigg, in his book *When God Becomes Goddess: The Transformation of American Religion*,[46] has reassured us that religion in America will not disappear but is in the "process of transformation." "Significant elements of traditional religious belief and practice [that is, biblical Twoism or theism] are passing away, but a new kind of religiosity is poised to take its place."[47] But it is not new. It is the old Oneist Gnosticism, but is now hailed as a new breath of fresh air for those dissatisfied with biblical orthodoxy.

One of these, often hailed as the most influential American New Testament scholar of the twentieth century, is James Robinson. Once a Bible-believing Reformed Christian, Robinson became the director of the translation project of the Coptic Gnostic texts. In his introduction to this weighty volume, Robinson has many negative things to say about Christian orthodoxy and many positive things to say about the future impact of these ancient texts on the spirituality of our contemporary world.

Negatively. Robinson dismissed the second- and third-century Christian bishops who opposed the anti-Christian character of Gnosticism as prejudiced and "short-sighted," as mere "myopic heresy-hunters."[48] This is still how liberals try to portray historic Christianity—closed-minded and bigoted, just as President Obama in 2009 characterized those opposing homosexuality as holding on to "worn arguments and old attitudes."[49] Actually, where the nature of human life is concerned, there is little that is new.

Positively. With obvious delight, Robinson presented these newly found texts as an attractive, timeless, and thus immediately applicable "answer to the human dilemma." Robinson declared that the newly found Gnostic library had "much in common with primitive Christianity."[50] This was the beginning of an attempt to totally revise our understanding of early Christianity along Gnostic-pagan lines.

Along with a well-funded cohort of radical scholars associated with the Jesus Seminar, Robinson attempted to prove that the

Gospel of Thomas predates the canonical Gospels. This massive, extremely hypothetical reconstruction of Christian origins lies behind the new optimism of so-called progressive Christianity, exemplified in the writing of Harvard professor and liberal Baptist Harvey Cox, who claims that we are now entering "the Age of the Spirit," fortunately leaving behind "the Age of Belief."[51] Cox argues that "the Gnostic texts show that a wide variety of different versions of Christianity, not just one, flourished in the early centuries. The discovery of Thomas opened the door to a refreshing new understanding of the first centuries of Christian life." The euphoric Cox goes on to say that this new age of spirituality celebrates the "move to horizontal transcendence" or "a turn to immanence, . . . a rediscovery of the sacred in the immanent," where experience of "faith" from all the religions is an important part of the Spirit's new work—"a new Pentecost."[52]

The fact is, a number of biblical Christian scholars have done serious work to show that this reconstruction of early Christianity is without historical value, and is driven only by a radical theological agenda.[53] Also, all these speculative attempts to insert Gnosticism into early Christianity smash against the solid rock of 1 Corinthians 15:1–11, which contains the earliest Christian creed we possess, coming directly from the Jerusalem church of the mid- to late 30s of the Christian era.[54]

BEFORE WE MOVE ON

+ What present-day conflict do we see between Christian orthodoxy and repackaged Gnosticism? How are Gnostics attempting to revise our understanding of early Christianity? How have biblical Christian scholars countered these claims?

+ What is the "new Pentecost" described by Harvey Cox? Why is this event so exciting for Gnostics? How is this different from the Pentecost described in Scripture?

THE PAGAN HEART OF TODAY'S CULTURE

Robinson also affirms that the Nag Hammadi Coptic Gnostic texts "have much in common with eastern religions and with holy men of all times."[55] In this Robinson is correct. Gnosticism *is* one particular form of Eastern, pagan, polytheistic religion, and in particular a "Christian" expression of the so-called mystery religions of the Roman Empire. Clearly, this ancient spirituality would fuel the growing interest in the contemporary interfaith syncretism that now seeks to unite all the religions, so Robinson also affirms that "these texts have much in common with . . . the counter-culture movements coming from the 1960s."[56]

Indeed, the introduction of these texts happened as the hippies were going east and the gurus were coming west to "liberate" sex and spirituality. It is truly fascinating that the discovery and dissemination of the Gnostic texts coincide with the dominance in the West of both occultic Jungian psychology (Jung was a Gnostic) and the 1960s cultural revolution whose radical agenda has become public policy in the America of the twenty-first century.

In the important area of psychology, the ground for Gnostic spirituality had been prepared by Freud, who radically undermined the entire Enlightenment project by his revelation that below or beyond the rational mind existed an overwhelmingly potent repository of nonrational forces that did not readily submit either to rational analysis or to conscious manipulation. His pupil Carl Jung took things much further, claiming to discover in the human psyche a collective unconscious common to all human beings and structured according to powerful archetypal paranormal principles of worldwide paganism.[57]

In other words, the modern Gnostics (such as Carl Jung and James Robinson) immediately saw the value of these texts as fitting perfectly with the "progressive" culture of pagan Eastern spirituality that has developed since the 1960s.

A contemporary Wiccan priestess of Isis, Caitlín Matthews, agrees: "Gnosticism serves most admirably as a bridge for paganism to infiltrate Christianity [in our time]."[58] She announces "the Second Coming of the Goddess," that is, the "Sophianic Millennium," the era of goddess-blessing and worship when all peoples and faiths will be united. For this to happen, the monotheistic Jahweh must be silenced as an era of polytheism approaches.

BEFORE WE MOVE ON

✢ What factors coincided with the discovery of the Gnostic texts known as the Nag Hammadi Gnostic Coptic texts? What are the philosophical connections between these cultural developments? How did Gnosticism serve as a bridge for paganism into Christianity?

POLYTHEISM

As we pass from Gnosticism to polytheism, it is worthy of note that a modern authority on polytheism, Jordan Paper, observes: "The first Christian heresies, labeled Gnosticism, tended toward polytheism."[59] Effectively, we are dealing with variants of the same theme.

Polytheism is as old as the hills and "covers all the cultures of the world."[60] It includes all the nonbiblical religions as far apart as Buddhism, Native American shamanism, and Chinese, Manchurian, Hawaiian, and ancient Greek and Roman religions, because, says Paper, polytheism "fits the human mind and experience so comfortably."[61] It is "the human cultural norm . . . reflecting human nature," whereas, says Paper, monotheism is "contrary" to human nature.[62] This is certainly true. The polytheist goes within to meet the gods. The theist goes outside the self to meet the God of utter transcendence.

So this ancient system is the direct opposite of biblical faith, as Paper recognizes: "Monotheism and polytheism are ideologically in opposition."[63] Obviously, the idea of one God versus many gods represents two clearly contradictory confessions, but the difference has to do not only with number, but with kind. The God of monotheism is the transcendent Other, the Creator beyond the creation; the gods of polytheism are immanent within creation, and "creation" and human beings share their divine nature.[64] According to Paper, for the polytheist, the multiplicity of gods is an advantage—"the more the better . . . [for] one has nothing to lose by making offerings to every available deity."[65] This is especially true because the deities are not assumed to be omnipotent, nor are they always successful with regard to human requests. Some indeed may lose their power altogether.[66] This is doubtless why polytheism contains both unitary and multiple understandings of the divine. In Hinduism, which has 250 million gods, Shiva is often understood as the supreme god. Moreover, in spite of this multitude of deities present in the various Hindu traditions, they all share an essential commonality of the Great Spirit. Thus, many gods and one Great Spirit can be found side by side.[67] And while this Great Spirit can sometimes be called "the Creator," polytheistic traditions "tend not to have creation myths"[68] because polytheism is not interested in the creation event.

BEFORE WE MOVE ON

+ Polytheism is a major feature of religions found all over the world. Why does Jordan Paper argue that this is the case? In what way does the author agree with him?

+ What does Paper see as an advantage to polytheism? Pragmatically speaking, what are some disadvantages for the polytheist?

Could such an ancient "primitive" religion find traction in the sophisticated twenty-first century? In 1974 in "Christian" America, we witnessed the publication of an oddly titled book— *The New Polytheism: The Rebirth of the Gods and Goddesses*. When I arrived in the United States from Britain in 1964 for theological education, I was immediately asked to read books by American "death of God" theologians. We understood the "death of God" as a liberal attack on the God of the Bible, part of the secular-humanist victory over religious superstition. But one of these "theologians," David Miller, professor of religion at Syracuse University and an apparent secular atheist, was clearly embracing "religious superstition," and wrote the book with the provocative title I cited above. What on earth is going on here? He stated with great foresight that at the funeral of the God of the Bible, we would see the rebirth of the gods and goddesses of ancient Greece and Rome:[69]

> The announcement of the death of God was the obituary of a useless single-minded and one-dimensional norm of a civilization that has been predominantly monotheistic, not only in its religion, but also in its politics, its history, its social order, its ethics, and its psychology. When released from the tyrannical imperialism of monotheism by the death of God, man has the opportunity of discovering new dimensions hidden in the depths of reality's history.[70]

As an interesting side note, the "new polytheist" David Miller worked closely with those who were promoting the revival of Gnosticism in the church and the culture, all associated with Eranos, a study center in Switzerland devoted to the study of the psychotherapy and pagan ideology of C. G. Jung.

In 1995 Jean Houston, a self-identified Jungian who counseled Hillary Clinton (then in the White House) and helped her to channel the spirit of Eleanor Roosevelt, observed that our present society was in a state of both "breakdown and breakthrough—... what I call a whole system transition ... requir[ing] a new alignment that only myth can bring."[71] These were the myths of polytheism. Houston published a book that year, *The Passion of Isis and Osiris*, proposing as the saving myth for the modern world the story of the Egyptian goddess Isis, goddess of magic and the underworld. "Now open your eyes," she has said, "and look at all the gods in hiding"[72]—in America!

Houston the polytheist is now a senior consultant for the United Nations Development Program established in 2000 at the Millennium Summit, now in 166 countries. UNDP sponsors Houston's work in leadership training, which takes her to all the underdeveloped countries to teach young leaders "social artistry," reconnecting them with their old ancestral polytheistic myths. The mythologically wise community will be the basis of the planetary community.

Jordan Paper can explain the essence of polytheism, having been a monotheist who became a committed polytheist. Here is his testimony: "What is a good Jewish boy doing writing a polytheistic theology?" He answers:

[Because] the Judaism of my childhood . . . was a Judaism of ritual . . . [in which] the God disclosed to me was one who looked for any excuse to punish, but there was no corollary reward. . . . Thus, I could live in fear of God or ignore Him. I chose the latter. . . . Coming across a slim anthology of Buddhist sutra excerpt . . . [it] captivated me. It did not simply fill a spiritual void; the early sutras made absolute sense to me, as they seemed to analyze my own experiences.[73]

Paper, a recognized scholar of world religions, analyzing their structures in what he calls a "Eurocentric" scientific manner, now claims to have written, at the end of his career, the first systematic apologetic for polytheistic theology—*as a believer!* He makes a fascinating admission—that his primary understanding of the deities comes not from study but from direct experience with them. "Real understanding came from cultural participation rather than books[,] . . . vision quests . . . where I was given understandings."[74] Mystical, occult experience of the deities, as he affirms, in effect, is the real source of polytheistic theology.[75]

This is the attractiveness and power of polytheism. As part of the natural world, "people come to know the deities directly." Hence the multiplicity of deities, because "people with differing personalities and experiences need differing deities."[76] The spirit-deities are many because they represent the forces of nature, such as sky and earth, male and female, yin and yang, and because nature is considered a complex, living, spiritual organism, with animal, plant, and even mineral spirits. The relationships with the deities are "reciprocal,"[77] because the spirits in nature seek a relationship with living humans. The polytheist seeks shamanistic "personal relations with cosmic forces,"[78] through either "divination" or "spirit possession."[79] Techniques of initiation into altered states of consciousness require physical stimuli such as sweat lodges[80] or the taking of drugs such as peyote,[81] plus the use of spiritually charged physical images (what the Bible calls "carved image[s]," Ex. 20:4) of the deities as a focal point of devotion.[82] While Gnosticism is often only implicitly occultic, clearly polytheism is openly and unapologetically involved in the worship of demons. Certainly, like Gnosticism and all the other pagan traditions, polytheism has no notion of genuine evil and thus seeks, for personal advantage, to join the opposites of good and evil to eliminate all notions of guilt. According to Paper, polytheistic cultures tend not to have a concept of evil, nor of the biblical understanding of the relationship between God and the devil.[83]

Polytheism also gives rise to polysexuality, for since there is no Creator, and thus no creational norms, human-divine beings decide what sexuality is right for them. So much is homosexuality a part of religious paganism that historical scholarship agrees that in polytheistic cults throughout time and space, the shaman or priest is homosexual.[84]

Polytheism is alive today under many guises. Mormonism is polytheistic inasmuch as the Mormon god was once a human, and human beings will become gods ruling over their own planets. Also, just as the ancient Gnostics called Jahweh a demon, so one of the leaders of Mormonism, Brigham Young, said that the "Christian God is the Mormon's Devil and the Mormon's Devil is the Christian God."[85] I witnessed polytheism in action at the Parliament of the World's Religions in Chicago in 1993, where eight thousand delegates from 125 different religions locked elbows and danced around a vast ballroom, celebrating the deep unity of all their gods.

BEFORE WE MOVE ON

✦ What did the "death of God" movement attack? What did David Miller predict would follow the "death" of the God of the Bible? Why?

✦ What makes the experiential focus that we see in the stories of Jean Houston and Jordan Paper so appealing?

✦ Other than a plurality of gods, what do polytheistic religions have in common? What is a difference between polytheism and Gnosticism?

THE PERENNIAL PHILOSOPHY: A BRIDGE BETWEEN THESE THREE *ISMS*

We have examined these three systems of thought in their essence as separate systems, and have noted a few crossover themes. Now we need to see how they have become deeply intertwined in our time and the reason for their coming together—found in an explanation that is both ancient and surprisingly contemporary.

In Romans 1:25, the apostle Paul makes a luminously simple yet profound statement. He states that there are only two types of spirituality: (1) worship and service of nature-creation, which I have called pagan Oneism, in which everything shares the same divine nature and all is therefore one, and (2) worship and service of the Creator, which I have called God-honoring Twoism, which emphasizes two kinds of existence, that of the Creator and that of the creation. Into these two possibilities, if Paul is right, all human systems can be eventually fitted.

Certainly all the world's non-Christian religions can be fitted into Paul's scheme, because they believe themselves to hold the same beliefs—as the Parliament of the World's Religions, mentioned above, affirmed—and have a term for it: *the Perennial Philosophy.* Peter Occhiogrosso, author of the six-hundred-page encyclopedia on world religions called *The Joy of Sects,* shows that behind the many seemingly antagonistic expressions of the world's religions, there is a deep level of agreement "which is not spoken of by their mainstream purveyors."[86] "This is the level," he says, "sometimes referred to as the Perennial Philosophy." He goes on: "Under and through each of the great traditions runs a stream—. . . a single stream that feeds each of these traditions from a single source[,] . . . the Perennial Philosophy."[87] Aldous Huxley, inventor of the term *Perennial Philosophy,* describes it as a belief system that recognizes

a divine Reality substantial to the world of things and lives and minds; the psychology that finds in the soul something similar to, or even identical with, divine Reality; the ethic that places man's final end in the knowledge of the immanent and transcendent Ground of all being—the thing is immemorial and universal. Rudiments of the Perennial Philosophy may

THE PAGAN HEART OF TODAY'S CULTURE

be found among the traditionary lore of primitive peoples in every region of the world, and in its fully developed forms it has a place in every one of the higher religions.[88]

Huxley calls this "the Highest Common Factor," which holds all the religions together.[89] Stephan Hoeller, bishop of the Ecclesia Gnostica of Los Angeles, places Gnosticism within this large category when he observes: "In his 1947 work *The Perennial Philosophy*, Aldous Huxley promulgated a kind of gnosis that was in effect a mystery reserved for elites, revealed at the dawn of history and handed down through various religious traditions, where it still maintains itself in spite of its ostensible incompatibility with the official dogmas of those traditions."[90]

Not only Gnosticism but the great Eastern religion of Hindusim can be added to this perennialist tradition. The religion scholar Philip Goldberg, documenting how modern America is turning to Hindu spirituality, justifies the religious synthesis taking place in our time by setting it precisely in the context of perennialism. He states that "perennialism arose from the frequent observation that the esoteric or mystical components of religious traditions—as opposed to exotic ritual, doctrine, ethics, and the like—call forth strikingly similar descriptions of reality, across cultures and regardless of era." The common factor, says Goldberg, is the mystical experience of oneness.[91]

BEFORE WE MOVE ON

+ Read Romans 1:25. What two kinds of spirituality are described in this verse? What does the author of this booklet call them? What is the key distinction between them?

+ Now that we have read more on this topic, would you revise your description of the Perennial Philosophy? If so, how? In the paragraph from Aldous Huxley, what words,

phrases, and ideas do you see that have also appeared in previous sections?
+ How does the Perennial Philosophy fit with the author's concept of Oneism?

According to the pagan myth, the natural world is all there is. This is the meaning of Huxley's phrase, quoted above, "a divine Reality substantial to the world." So there is "divinity," but it is found as an element of the world. There is nothing outside the created cosmos of a different order of being. Therefore, divine nature is alone worthy of worship. "Myths" must be invented to bestow divine status on Mother Nature—hence the vast network of goddess-worship in the ancient world. Paul attributes this concept to "teachings of demons" (1 Tim. 4:1), because the demons teach that the so-called Creator is evil or nonexistent.

Any system of thought that attempts to describe the world exclusively by the world is in principle Oneist. Take, for example, the Jewish philosopher Spinoza (1632–77). He was accused of atheism because he declared that there was only "one substance" in the entirety of being, that there is nothing outside of creation, and that "God" was merely the laws of nature. Likewise, Stephen Hawking, the British physicist, identified God with the laws of nature, and Einstein spoke of God but explicitly endorsed Spinoza.[92] Thus, atheism and rationalistic humanism are in that sense Oneist.[93] They, like their *spiritual* cousins, make no place for a transcendent, personal Creator, and so share at the deepest level the same view of reality as very spiritual but Oneist systems.[94] It is interesting that the modern atheists in the news attack Twoistic theism, the God of the Bible, but find few or no problems with the New Spirituality. A contemporary French atheist attacks exclusively "*la métaphysique judéo-chrétienne*" ("the Judeo-Christian metaphysics"), that is, the Creator God who is distinct from his creation.[95] Other forms of spirituality are no threat to atheism because they all share the same Oneist worldview. This is the conclusion of the atheistic philosopher Mitchell Silver, who teaches philosophy at the University of Massachusetts, Boston. Silver examines the "new" Jewish spirituality based on mystical kabbalah in its relationship to atheism,[96] in particular the spirituality of Michael Lerner, who as an adviser to First Lady Hillary Clinton proposed his "politics of meaning."[97] Silver is a thoroughgoing atheist who states openly that "the new god [as opposed to the old god of biblical theism] may be the only god that has a ghost of a chance of being believed by moderns."[98] Nevertheless, he concludes that "the new god" is not so "new," since it echoes and develops religious thought of Hinduism. He shows that this not-so-new "new god" is no more useful than a belief in no god to describe the nature of human existence. The final judgment of Silver is most telling. The new god of modern spirituality (based on ancient pagan spirituality) "is so thoroughly naturalistic that a godless nature can be expected to perform about as well as a godly one."[99] The "godless" and the newly "godly" can surely get along. The BBC journalist and successful author John Humphrys observes that the secular West "is losing its reticence about religion."[100] Thus we enter the era of the postsecular. The postsecular, created in large part by the postmodern destruction of secular rationalism, involves "a renewed openness to questions of the spirit while retaining the secular habits of critical thought."[101] But the ensuing religion, according to philosopher Mike King, will reject both closed-minded atheism and "the old religion" (Christianity). Rather, the coming religion will be a mix of "the religious Left," "the New Age," and Eastern "mysticism."[102] This has "apocalyptic" implications.

Before we move on

+ What belief unites spiritual and secular Oneists? In what ways do they hold the same view of nature? In what ways does this view differ?

+ How have postmodernism and postsecularism prepared the West to embrace Oneism?

THE COMING SYNTHESIS

Is this "tale of three *isms*" just a fortuitous merging of interesting philosophical or religious streams of thought that Christians should understand? Or are we witnessing a powerful urge to reconstruct the world that has languished so long under the sway of the biblical worldview? Is the threat to secular humanism not a brand-new system of religious thought but rather a modern embrace of the ancient spirituality of the pre-Christian world? Has the reconstruction prepared by the deconstructive effects of postmodernism led to a revival of the age-old religions of Gnosticism and polytheism? Certainly this deeply religious occurrence helps to explain many of the surface changes in cultural ethical norms, for example, in marriage, childbirth, and sexual expression. These changes are not driven simply by Hollywood producers who push the envelope for box-office success. They are the inevitable results of a radical reinterpretation of the very nature of human existence. We can reasonably speak of the recent appearance of a pagan "apocalyptic" worldview that now claims to be the spiritual culmination of the long flow of Western history.

This is indeed the vision of the brilliant pagan philosopher Richard Tarnas. He senses the arrival of a "powerful crescendo"[103] as "many movements *gather now on the intellectual stage as if for some kind of climactic synthesis.*"[104]

In Tarnas's vast view:

> Platonic and Presocratic philosophy, Hermeticism, mythology, the mystery religions[,] ... Buddhist and Hindu[,] ... Gnosticism and the major esoteric traditions[, and] ... Neolithic European and Native American spiritual traditions . . . have re-emerged to play new roles in the current intellectual scene . . . for some kind of climactic synthesis . . . . A powerful crescendo can be sensed . . . uttered by the West's great thinkers and visionaries concerning an imminent shift in the ages.[105]

This syncretistic view certainly includes Gnosticism and polytheism. And now the occultic mystical Romantics of the present time have come out of left field to include modernity and postmodernity in their unifying vision. Ken Wilber, another powerful thinker in today's Oneist camp, states that "the Enlightenment did not fail but is merely incomplete."[106] He congratulates the modernists for having pioneered the achievement of "autonomy"—autonomy from *what* he does not say, but it is clearly autonomy from God the Creator, now considered an ancient, unbelievable myth. And now he invites them to go deeper into a holistic, religious understanding of everything.[107] In the same way, Tarnas finds a place for postmodernism, explicitly arguing that this "imaginal intuition" of contemporary holistic spirituality "incorporates the postmodern understanding of knowledge and yet goes beyond it."[108] Both Wilber and Tarnas see autonomous modernity, and its offspring, postmodernity, as necessary steps in the evolution of consciousness, leading humanity out of dependence on a "pre-rational, anthropomorphic, mythic God figure"[109] (that is, the transcendent Creator God of Scripture, for whom they have no place in their synthesis) into a freeing union of the self with spiritualized nature. According to Wilber, "What modernity differentiated, postmodernity must integrate."[110] Tarnas calls this coming event a synthesis of the Romantic[111] and the rational, or "the meeting of science and spirit."[112] Hence, "the imaginal intuition [he is referring here to rediscovered mystical occultic, paranormal spirituality] is not a subjective distortion [as the science of the past once dismissed it], but is the human fulfillment of reality's essential wholeness," a wholeness that had been rent asunder by dualistic thinking, whether by atheism or theism.[113] This "intuition" reveals the powerful return of nature. Says Tarnas:

> The human spirit does not merely prescribe nature's phenomenal order; rather the spirit of nature brings forth its *own* order through the human mind when that mind is employing its full complement of faculties—intellectual, volitional, emotional, sensory, imaginative, aesthetic, epiphanic.[114]

The skeptical modernists were using only part of their minds. The new postsecular Romantics are firing on all human cylinders. The interfaith expert Huston Smith, a self-described "perennialist," believes that science must "reestablish our link with the primordial tradition and embrace a more expansive view of ourselves and our place in nature. . . . Science can still play an important role in this new epistemology, but it will no longer be seen as the ultimate source of authority."[115] Ultimate authority will come from this "primordial tradition," showing us "our place in nature." In other words, ultimate authority will arise from the pagan Perennial Philosophy. The American Humanist Association, a classic bastion of atheism, has also understood this new religious moment and stated, without the least hint of embarrassment:

> The battle for humankind's future must be waged and won in the classroom by teachers who correctly perceive their

role as the *proselytizers of a new faith*: a religion of humanity that recognizes and respects the spark of . . . *divinity in every human being*. The classroom must and will become an arena of conflict between the old and the new—the rotting corpse of Christianity . . . and the new faith of humanism.[116]

The humanistic prose now throbs with spirituality, explaining what happened to Mikhail Gorbachev, the last leader of the Soviet Empire, and a pure product of the atheistic Marxist system. Gorbachev now preaches a form of religious conversion:

> We need to find a paradigm that will integrate all the achievements of the human mind and human action, irrespective of which ideology or political movement can be credited with them. This paradigm can only be based on the common values that humankind has developed over many centuries. The search for a new paradigm should be a search for synthesis, for what is common to and unites people, countries, and nations, rather than what divides them. The search for such a synthesis can succeed if the following conditions are met. . . . We must return to the well-known human values that were embodied in the ideals of world religions and also in the socialist ideas that inherited much from those values.[117]

The Marxist materialist has become a mystic!

At the end of his massive work *The Passion of the Western Mind*, Tarnas concludes, with the eloquence of a scholar and the ardor of a believer: "For the deepest passion of the Western mind has been to reunite with the ground of its own being."[118]

BEFORE WE MOVE ON

+ How are changes in cultural ethical norms a reflection of the growing power of polytheism to reconstruct the world once postmodernism has *de*constructed it?

+ What "climactic synthesis" does Richard Tarnas see on the horizon? What are the signs of this dramatic movement?
+ How are modernism and postmodernism being synthesized? What do Oneists owe to modernism? What roles do they see for these two ideologies?
+ What is the ultimate authority for Oneists? Why might even Mikhail Gorbachev and the American Humanist Association embrace this authority? What vision do they have for the future?

THE CHRISTIAN RESPONSE

Christian, be advised. The Oneist reunion with nature (its "own being") and the Western embrace of the Hindu concept of *Advaita*[119] ("not two")[120] in all areas of life, including the philosophical, religious, political, and sexual, represent a massive apologetic challenge to the rising generation of Christians in the years ahead. For the Oneists, Twoism is the enemy. As secular humanism "comes home" to its pagan spiritual, homocosmological roots, expressed in both Gnosticism and polytheism, in a strange admixture with postmodern subjectivism, two things at least are required of Christian believers:

+ A clear understanding of the coherence of this opposing spiritual Oneism, which comes in many forms, not just three; and
+ A clear affirmation of the glorious superiority of the world of Twoism and a fearless declaration of the gospel of reconciliation with the personal Creator, possible only through the atoning blood of Jesus, the sole Mediator between Creator and creature.

This saving truth is *the only system of thought* that Oneist vision-aries cannot integrate into their otherwise all-inclusive ideology. Twoism is the Achilles' heel of their "all-is-one" fantasy. Twoism must therefore be spoken of and lived out with love, courage, and coherent clarity before a hostile world progressively enveloped by the delusion of the unifying Oneist lie. And as Paul implied so long ago, the future confrontation will be between not simply thinkers but spiritual worshipers, the *worshipers* of creation and the *worshipers* of the Creator.

In this light, the following text from Deuteronomy, where God addresses the Israelites before they go into the Promised Land, gives long-term perspective for our present time:

> Therefore watch yourselves very carefully. Since you saw no form on the day that the LORD spoke to you at Horeb . . . , beware lest you act corruptly by making a carved image for yourselves, in the form of any figure . . . . Beware lest . . . when you see the sun and the moon and the stars, all the host of heaven, you bow down to them and serve them . . . . The LORD your God is a consuming fire, a jealous God. . . . The LORD is God; there is no other besides him. . . . The LORD is God in heaven above and on the earth beneath; there is no other. (Deut. 4:15–16, 19, 24, 35, 39)

It turns out that there are not three *isms*, or the many other *isms* of pagan thinking and practice that we could have described. There are only two. Thirty-five hundred years ago there were only two options—obeying the voice of the transcendent Creator (Two*ism*) and worshiping created things (One*ism*). At this level, nothing has changed.[121]

IN CONCLUSION

+ As you conclude this booklet, what have you learned about polytheism, Gnosticism, and postmodernism? Have you become aware of further ways that these ideologies influence you or people with whom you have contact? How have these ideologies permeated the culture you live in?

+ What is the author's call to Christians in the face of Oneism? Why is it so important for Twoists to hold fast to their beliefs?

+ What do we need to remember about God, particularly when we are tempted by Oneism?

+ Going forward, what are some practical ways in which you can live out Twoism "with love, courage, and coherent clarity"?

NOTES

1. See Mike King, *Postsecularism: The Hidden Challenge to Extremism* (Cambridge: James Clarke & Co., 2009); Simon During, "Toward the Postsecular," *PMLA: Publications of the Modern Language Association of America*, 120, 3 (May 2005).

2. King, *Postsecularism*, 5. King further adds that *postsecularism* includes both "pluralism" and "mysticism" (45), and joins "the religious left" and the "New Age" (47).

3. Crystal L. Downing, *How Postmodernism Serves (My) Faith* (Downers Grove, IL: IVP Academic, 2006), 36.

4. Richard J. Bernstein, ed., *Habermas and Modernity* (Oxford: Oxford University Press, 1985), 225.

5. Downing, *Postmodernism*, 26.

6. Richard Tarnas, *Passion of the Western Mind: Understanding Ideas That Have Shaped Our World View* (New York: Random House, 1991), 396. Richard Tarnas, Ph.D., is Distinguished Rockefeller Faculty, Professor of Philosophy and Psychology, at the California Institute of Integral Studies in San Francisco. He was formerly director of programs and education at Esalen Institute.

7. On the relation of orthodox Christianity and postmodernism, see Paul Kjoss Helseth, *"Right Reason" and the Princeton Mind: An Unorthodox Proposal* (Phillipsburg, NJ: P&R Publishing, 2010). See also Millard J. Erickson, Paul Kjoss

Helseth, and Justin Taylor, eds., *Reclaiming the Center: Confronting Evangelical Accommodation in Postmodern Times* (Wheaton, IL: Crossway, 2004).

8. See Tarnas, *Passion of the Western Mind*, 402, for the same observation.

9. Alister E. McGrath, *The Twilight of Atheism: The Rise and Fall of Disbelief in the Modern World* (New York: Doubleday, 2004), 230.

10. David Harvey, *The Condition of Postmodernity: An Enquiry into the Origins of Cultural Change* (Malden, MA: Blackwell Publishers, 1990), 358.

11. McGrath, *Twilight of Atheism*, xii.

12. See the obituary by Elaine Woo, "Jacques Derrida, 74: Intellectual Founded Controversial Deconstructionist Movement," *Los Angeles Times*, October 10, 2004.

13. Kevin J. Vanhoozer, *God, Scripture & Hermeneutics: First Theology* (Downers Grove, IL: InterVarsity Press, 2002), 211–12.

14. Richard Wolin, *The Seduction of Unreason: The Intellectual Romance with Fascism from Nietzsche to Postmodernism* (Princeton, NJ: Princeton University Press, 2004).

15. Christopher Partridge, *The Re-Enchantment of the West: Alternative Spiritualities, Sacralization, Popular Culture, and Occulture*, vol. 1 (London and New York: T&T Clark International, 2004), 4.

16. Ibid., 53.

17. Tarnas, *Passion of the Western Mind*, 436.

18. Partridge, *Re-Enchantment of the West*, 38–40.

19. Huston Smith, *Beyond the Postmodern Mind* (Wheaton, IL: Quest, 2003).

20. Peter Occhiogrosso, *The Joy of Sects* (New York: Doubleday, 1996), xvi.

21. See Prince Charles's opening speech at the 2006 conference "Tradition in the Modern World," convened by the "traditionalist journal" *Sacred Web* of the Temenos Academy. He is the Patron of the Temenos Academy. The *Temenos Academy Review* is the journal of the Academy and is the successor to the journal *Temenos*. HRH The Prince of Wales wrote that the Academy and its review are "committed both to the perennial philosophy and to the notion that Man is, at root, a spiritual creature with spiritual and intellectual needs which have to be nourished if we are to fulfill our potential." World Wisdom, "Life and Work of HRH Charles Windsor, The Prince of Wales," http://www.worldwisdom.com/public/authors/HRH-Charles-Windsor-Prince-of-Wales.aspx.

22. Francis A. Schaeffer, *The God Who Is There* (Downers Grove, IL: InterVarsity Press, 1968), 70. See also Francis A. Schaeffer, *Pollution and the*

Death of Man (Downers Grove, IL: InterVarsity Press, 1970); Os Guinness, *The Dust of Death: A Critique of the Counter Culture* (Downers Grove, IL: InterVarsity Press, 1973), 229, 281.

23. Peter Jones, *Stolen Identity: The Conspiracy to Reinvent Jesus* (Colorado Springs: Cook Communications, 2006).

24. Ibid., 196–200.

25. Gospel of Thomas, Saying 13, in James M. Robinson, ed., *The Nag Hammadi Library in English* (San Francisco: Harper and Row, 1977), 119.

26. Ibid., 108.

27. Jones, *Stolen Identity*, 165–66.

28. Elaine Pagels, "What Was Lost Is Found: A Wider View of Christianity and Its Roots," in *Secrets of the Code: The Unauthorized Guide to the Mysteries of the Da Vinci Code*, ed. Dan Burstein (New York: CDS Books, 2004), 100.

29. The two views blend into each other. See note 65.

30. Gospel of Thomas, 77. See also Saying 19 (in which Jesus speaks of stones' ministering to the disciples).

31. Hans Jonas, *The Gnostic Religion* (Boston: Beacon Press, 1958).

32. Kurt Rudolph, *Gnosis: The Nature and History of an Ancient Religion* (Edinburgh: T&T Clark, 1977), 276.

33. Ibid., 55.

34. Ibid., 58.

35. Quoted in ibid., 14.

36. Hippolytus, *Refutation of All Heresies*, 5:9:10. This would be an ancient example of the "Perennial Philosophy," which will be addressed below.

37. *The Thunder: Perfect Mind*, 16:6–7.

38. James Preston, "Goddess Worship: An Overview," in *The Book of the Goddess, Past and Present: An Introduction to Her Religion*, ed. Carl Olson (Prospect Heights, IL: Waveland, 2002), 38. Pheme Perkins, in an article in this same book, reflecting on *The Thunder: Perfect Mind*, says: "Like Isis, this female figure [whom she takes to be Sophia] claims to be behind all human wisdom." "Sophia and the Father-Mother: The Gnostic Goddess," in Olson, *Book of the Goddess*, 99.

39. See the description of Sophia in the program of the RE-Imagining Conference as "the place where the entire universe resides." American Family Association, "The RE-Imagining Conference: A Report," available at http://afajournal.org/1994/0594AFAJ.pdf.

40. Quoted in Monica Sjöö and Barbara Mor, *The Great Cosmic Mother: Rediscovering the Religion of the Earth* (San Francisco: HarperCollins, 1987), 253.

41. *Trimorphic Protennoia*, 45:3–4.

42. I deal at length with this subject of the Gnostic God in my book *Spirit Wars: Pagan Revival in Christian America* (Mukilteo, WA: Wine Press, 1997), 161–76.

43. *Sophia of Jesus Christ*, 112:19; 114:14–15.

44. *Trimorphic Protennoia*, 39:21; 40:23; 43:32; 43:35–44:2.

45. *Hypostasis of the Archons*, 95:8ff. Cf. *On the Origin of the World*, 103:25ff.

46. Richard Grigg, *When God Becomes Goddess: The Transformation of American Religion* (New York: Continuum, 1995), 22.

47. Ibid.

48. Robinson, *Nag Hammadi Library*, 1.

49. NewsBusters.org (July 1, 2009), http://www.bpnews.net/BPnews .asp?ID=30803.

50. Robinson, *Nag Hammadi Library*, 3.

51. Harvey Cox, *The Future of Faith* (New York: HarperCollins, 2009), 165.

52. Ibid.

53. See, for instance, Andreas J. Köstenberger and Michael J. Kruger, *The Heresy of Orthodoxy*, foreword by I. Howard Marshall (Wheaton, IL: Crossway, 2010); Charles E. Hill, *Who Chose the Gospels? Probing the Great Gospel Conspiracy* (Oxford: Oxford University Press, 2010); Mark S. Goodacre and Nicholas Perrin, *Questioning Q: A Multidimensional Critique* (Downers Grove, IL: InterVarsity Press, 2005).

54. See truthXchange, "Dr. Jones Explains the Gnostic Gospel," online video, available at http://truthxchange.com/media/2011/06/02/dr-jones-explains -the-gnostic-gospel/.

55. Robinson, *Nag Hammadi Library*, 1.

56. Ibid.

57. Tarnas, *Passion of the Western Mind*, 385.

58. Caitlín Matthews, *Sophia, Goddess of Wisdom: The Divine Feminine from Black Goddess to World-Soul* (London: Aquarian Press/Harper Collins, 1992), 67, notes that "the strong character of Isis the Goddess became the Sophianic touchstone of . . . Gnosticism."

59. Jordan D. Paper, *The Deities Are Many: A Polytheistic Theology* (Albany, NY: State University of New York Press, 2005), 127. See also Michael York, *Pagan Theology: Paganism as a World Religion* (New York: New York University Press, 2003).

60. Paper, *Deities Are Many*, 4–5.
61. Ibid., 4.
62. Ibid., 104.
63. Ibid., 133.
64. Ibid., 128.
65. Ibid., 138.
66. Ibid., 139.
67. Ibid., 122.
68. Ibid., 114.
69. David LeRoy Miller, *The New Polytheism: The Rebirth of the Gods and Goddesses* (San Francisco: Harper, 1974), vii–x.
70. Ibid., vii. Beyond all the partisan politics, we are witnessing the public showdown of two competing worldviews.
71. Jean Houston, *The Passion of Isis and Osiris: A Gateway to Transcendent Love* (New York: Ballantine, 1995), 2 (emphasis added).
72. Jean Houston, *A Passion for the Possible: A Guide to Realizing Your True Potential* (San Francisco: HarperSanFrancisco, 1997), 20, quoted in James A. Herrick, *The Making of the New Spirituality: The Eclipse of the Western Religious Tradition* (Downers Grove, IL: InterVarsity Press, 2003), 177.
73. Paper, *Deities Are Many*, 6.
74. Ibid., 10.
75. This was also true of Carl Jung, who developed his transpersonal psychology from his encounters with the demonic spirit world. To learn more about this, see the video series of my lectures, *Only Two Religions* (Ligonier Ministries, 2014).
76. Paper, *Deities Are Many*, 13.
77. Ibid., 14.
78. Ibid., 34.
79. Ibid., 68.
80. Ibid., 26.
81. Ibid., 40.
82. Ibid., 84.
83. Ibid., 129.
84. See Peter Jones, "Androgyny: The Pagan Sexual Ideal," *Journal of the Evangelical Theological Society* 43, 3 (2000): 443–69.
85. *Journal of Discourses*, 5:331.
86. Occhiogrosso, *Joy of Sects*, xvi.

87. Ibid., xvi, xxi. The deep unity of these various religions is evident from the fact that Aldous Huxley in *The Perennial Philosophy* (New York: Harper & Brothers, 1945) quotes extensively from "mystics and spiritual masters of the Hindu, Buddhist, Taoist, Judaic, Christian and Islamic traditions." Occhiogrosso, *Joy of Sects*, xvi. Note that the common theme is mysticism.
88. Huxley, *Perennial Philosophy*, vii.
89. Ibid.
90. Stephan Hoeller, "What Is a Gnostic?" *Gnosis: A Journal of Western Inner Traditions* 23 (Spring 1992): 22.
91. Philip Goldberg, *American Veda: How Indian Spirituality Changed the West* (New York: Harmony Books, 2010), 11–12.
92. Mitchell Silver, *A Plausible God: Secular Reflections on Liberal Jewish Theology* (New York: Fordham University Press, 2006), 6.
93. In a formal sense, rabbinic Judaism and Islam are "Twoist," but their non-Trinitarian God denies to God the essential element of transcendent personhood. To be in any sense personal, their God is dependent on personal creatures, and is thus part of creation, as in all the pagan religions.
94. Suspicion about religion and the spiritual continues to exist. In the *Los Angeles Times* you can still read items such as this: "The same mechanisms that make us such successful social creatures make us vulnerable to creating supernatural entities with human social attributes. We ascribe to these gods, or God, thoughts, desires, attitudes, beliefs, intentions and communicative abilities that are turbocharged reflections of our human capacities." The Times' Opinion Staff, "In God We See Ourselves," *Los Angeles Times*, July 26, 2011, Opinion L.A. section.
95. See Philippe Serradit, "La montée de l'athéisme contemporain," *La Revue Réformée* 259, 62 (Juillet 2011): 21.
96. Silver, *Plausible God*.
97. Michael Lerner, *Jewish Renewal* (New York: Putnam, 1994); Michael Lerner, *Spirit Matters* (Charlottesville, VA: Hampton Roads, 2000).
98. Silver, *Plausible God*, 10.
99. Ibid., 47.
100. John Humphrys, *In God We Doubt: Confessions of a Failed Atheist* (London: Hodder & Stoughton, 2007), quoted in King, *Postsecularism*, 121.
101. King, *Postsecularism*, 105.
102. Ibid., 45, 47.
103. Tarnas, *Passion of the Western Mind*, 411.

104. Ibid., 403 (emphasis added).
105. Ibid., 403, 411.
106. Ken Wilber, *Sex, Ecology, Spirituality: The Spirit of Evolution* (Boston: Shambhala, 2000), 401.
107. Ibid., 400.
108. Tarnas, *Passion of the Western Mind*, 435.
109. Wilber, *Sex, Ecology, Spirituality*, 404. Wilber compares this unworthy divine being of the Bible that modernity rejected to the "trans-rational, non-anthropomorphic, super-conscient Godhead" that it should have embraced but did not—until now!
110. Ibid., 403.
111. Tarnas, *Passion of the Western Mind*, 373, explains what he means by Romanticism: "God was rediscovered in Romanticism—not the God of orthodoxy or deism but of mysticism, pantheism, and immanent cosmic process; not the juridical monotheistic patriarch but a divinity more ineffably mysterious, pluralistic, all-embracing, neutral, or even feminine in gender; not an absentee creator but a numinous creative force within nature and within the human spirit."
112. For another version of this new understanding of Western history, see King, *Postsecularism*. King argues that Western Enlightenment was a failed religious revolution. The true goal of the Enlightenment philosophers was to move Western culture from a devotional religious context (that is, Christianity) that denied the world to a context that emphasized direct knowledge, or mysticism, and embraced the life processes of nature. This, of course, was true of Hegel, one of the major figures often associated with the Enlightenment. On this, see Glenn Alexander Magee, *Hegel and the Hermetic Tradition* (Ithaca, NY: Cornell University Press, 2001). King argues that the project failed, resulting in a split between "devotional traditionalists" (the church) and an "'autistic' secular scientific community" that cannot discern the sacred or deeper dimensions of experience. King, *Postsecularism*, 44. Now, of course, the secularists are finding their way back to the original "religious" project. At the beginning you might say that the Enlightenment secular humanists were indeed Christian apostates, spiritual orphans whose goal was to undermine faith in an alien, divine word from God, but who lost their place in the world. Coming home to apostate spirituality now doubtless looks attractive. See

also Ken Wilber, *The Marriage of Sense and Soul: Integrating Science and Religion* (New York: Broadway Books, 1998), chaps. 11–12.

113. He means the two kinds of dualistic thinking: the rationalistic, skeptical approach of modern science, a kind of apostasy from its Christian roots, and the dualistic thinking of biblical Twoism, distinguishing between the Creator and the creature.

114. Tarnas, *Passion of the Western Mind*, 435. You find this prediction of the coming "synthesis" in Julian Huxley (brother of Aldous, mentioned above), past head of UNESCO. In 1947, he spoke of two opposing world-views: "You may categorize the two philosophies as . . . individualism versus collectivism or as the American versus the Russian . . . or as capitalism versus communism, or as Christianity versus Marxism. Can these opposites be reconciled, this antithesis be resolved in a higher synthesis? I believe . . . this can happen . . . through the inexorable dialectic of evolution." http://www.crossroad.to/Quotes/globalism/julian-huxley.htm, quoted in Linda Kimball, "Hegel's Dialectic: Erasing Christianity through the Psycho-Political 'Consensus Process,'" *RenewAmerica*, March 15, 2010.

115. Scott London, review of *Beyond the Post-Modern Mind*, by Huston Smith, http://www.scottlondon.com/reviews/hustonsmith.html.

116. Quoted in Frances Adeney, "Some Schools Are Looking East for Answers," *Moody Monthly*, May 1982, 19 (emphasis added).

117. Mikhail Gorbachev, *The Search for a New Beginning: Developing a New Civilization* (San Francisco: HarperSan Francisco, 1995), quoted in http://www.worldtrans.org/whole/gorbachev.html.

118. Tarnas, *Passion of the Western Mind*, 443.

119. See Goldberg, *American Veda*. Goldberg, a Jewish intellectual and convert to Hinduism, in this book quotes Lisa Miller, "We Are All Hindus Now," *Newsweek*, August 14, 2009, and informs us: "Large numbers of Americans have arrived at a worldview consistent with the principle articulated in the ancient *Rig Veda*, which she [Miller] translated as 'Truth is One, but the sages speak of it by many names.'" According to Goldberg, "America is engaged in a reconfiguring of the sacred, comparable to the Great Awakenings of the 18th century." Goldberg, *American Veda*, 5.

120. This Hindu term, which describes what Oneism is not (namely, it is not Twoist biblical faith), is becoming a popular notion, even among self-identifying evangelical Christians. Sally Morganthaler, who has lectured

on "leadership" at many evangelical schools, such as Denver Seminary, Fuller Theological Seminary, Gordon-Conwell Theological Seminary, Oral Roberts University, Regent University, and Biblical Theological Seminary in Hatfield, Pennsylvania, is now exploring "the convergence of a developmental view of life (evolutionary) and spirituality . . . and an accelerating trend toward *holism* (*the both/and*)." The Advent of Evolutionary Christianity, http://evolutionarychristianity.com/blog/speaker-bios/ (emphasis added). This thinking fits so easily with the Oneist synthesis proposed by Tarnas, and it is not without interest to note that many Emergent leaders, with whom Morganthaler collaborates, are enthusiastically reading the Oneist evolutionary theories of Buddhist Ken Wilber.

121. For an exposition of Oneism and Twoism, see Peter Jones, *One or Two: Seeing a World of Difference* (Escondido, CA: Main Entry Editions, 2010).

ALSO FROM PETER JONES

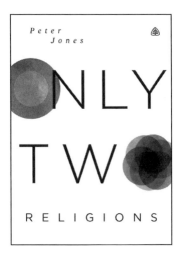

AVAILABLE AUGUST 2014

If you survey the religious landscape of modern culture, you will encounter an astonishingly diverse range of views. But beneath the surface, these seemingly disparate spiritualities share a common worldview, one that is radically opposed to the Christian faith. In this series, join Dr. Peter Jones as he examines the worldview and fundamental religious convictions that drive modern culture. He demonstrates that in the final analysis, there can be only two religions—worship of the Creator and worship of creation. By better understanding the present cultural context, you will be equipped to articulate the Christian faith and worldview more clearly to a world in need of redemption.

DVD: $48 • CD: $31
A&V Download: $24
Study Guide: $8